T0380827

PHOTOGRAPHS OF GRATITUDE

Journey Beyond Depression Through Photography

CAROL FLINN

Photography by Robin Flinn

Balboa Press books may be ordered through booksellers or by contacting:

Balboa Press
A Division of Hay House
1663 Liberty Drive
Bloomington, IN 47403
www.balboapress.com
1 (877) 407-4847

ISBN: 978-1-9822-0417-4 (sc)
ISBN: 978-1-9822-0418-1 (e)

Library of Congress Control Number: 2018905797

Print information available on the last page.

Balboa Press rev. date: 07/03/2018

BALBOA
PRESS
A DIVISION OF HAY HOUSE

DEDICATION

To those who struggle to find simplicity and light
in the midst of chaos and darkness.

"There are only two ways to live your life. One is as though nothing is a miracle. The other is as though everything is a miracle."

– Albert Einstein

"If the only prayer you ever say in your whole life is "thank you", that would suffice."

– Meister Eckhart

CONTENTS

INTRODUCTION

Photography savors split-second slices of one's reality. In a quest for beauty and predictable patterns, Robin used her pocket sized point and shoot camera to capture a new reality and recreate her life. Her photography became a vehicle for her journey from depression to gratitude … from a life of looking back to a life of here and now.

Depression is dark, focused on self, looking in and looking back. Throughout her life, Robin was oftentimes caught in a downward spiral of negativity and despair despite her persistent struggle to find meaning and a place of belonging in the world.

With the gentle nudging of a rescue dog named "Falcon," Robin began taking early morning walks in the parks of her Boston neighborhood. She developed a daily practice of gratitude by identifying, with intention, "what can I appreciate today, what can I be grateful for today?" She began seeking out beauty and color to combat the darkness, and the simplicity of patterns to quiet the chaos of her emotions.

Robin took her practice of gratitude one step further by asking, "what can I share today?" Photography became her means to capture the essence of what she appreciated, and she began posting photos daily on Facebook as a "journal of gratitude." In response, her friends expressed how much the photos made them smile and brought them joy. In one person's words,

> "Robin takes photos of everyday sights that are available for anyone to see. Her eye captures the essence of the everyday and then frames it in beauty, color, and joy. She takes the ordinary and gifts it back to us in a way that shows us how to appreciate the simplicity and patterns of life."

Other friends used words like "gorgeous," "lovely," "amazing," "unbelievable," "incredible," "spectacular," and "daily joy" to describe what she shared.

Still others commented with these words,

> "So incredibly beautiful and weird at the same time."
> "I love the way you see the details of a thing."
> "Looks like underwater photography ... lovely."
> "Love this shot, I can literally feel the mist on my skin."
> "Your photos bring sunlight into an occasionally dark world"
> "This should be hanging on someone's wall somewhere, like a Chinese watercolor."
> "You are a genius with a camera ... you keep amazing me."

Robin's individual approach to dealing with depression brought her to a particular style of photography. She did not take a class or learn specific techniques. She just came to it naturally. She had long been drawn to Buddhism as a spiritual practice, with the emphasis on here and now, the impermanence of everything, non-attachment, and selflessness. As she explored the field of photography, she discovered "Miksang," a form of contemplative photography developed out of Buddhist teachings, which uses mindful meditation with visual perceptions as the object of attention rather than watching one's breath. Robin also discovered the genre of minimalist photography, a simplistic style that keeps compositional elements to a minimum while capturing the essence of an object.

Both Miksang and minimalist photography resonated with Robin on a very deep level. Her desire to develop a daily practice of gratitude moved her to experience life in a new way by seeing the essence of her subject without overlays of meaning, judgment, value, or interpretation. With every photo, she created a venue for being present and capturing the purity of a moment.

Robin described her approach as follows,

> "I try to find the spectacular in the ordinary. I look at shapes, lines, patterns, symmetry, and for a splash of color to add to the mix. It is a different way of seeing, a quiet meditation in the present, and a path on grace."

As Robin broadened her circle of friends and developed her art, she found what she had been searching for her entire life … a place of belonging in the world and meaning to her existence.

Robin's "journal of gratitude" has resulted in a collection of remarkable photography. Because the photos come out of her camera with minimal post-processing, there is a pureness and honesty to her work. There is also solitude. Regardless of where she is or whom she is with, when she stops to take a photo, she is alone … fully connected to her subject, whether it is a flower, a ripple in the water, or a chalk drawing on the sidewalk. In this aloneness at that moment of the shoot, there is serenity and peace.

In a masterful book, *"If You Want to Write,"* Brenda Ueland described the creative impulse by using the following quotes from the letters of the painter Van Gogh.

"We take beautiful walks together… it is very beautiful here, if one only has an open and simple eye without any beams in it … but if one has that, it is beautiful everywhere."

"The world only concerns me in so far as I feel a certain debt and duty towards it and out of gratitude want to leave some souvenir in the shape of drawings or pictures, not made to please a certain tendency in art but to express sincere human feeling."

So it is with Robin. Her photos are intended to reveal beauty in the ordinary and to inspire connection and wonderment with life. It is Robin's hope that her photography will bring peace and joy to those who are struggling and inspire others to let go of the past and move on into a future of their choosing.

In Robin's words,

"I share them in gratitude and with the importance of staying in the present. Enjoy this day with those you love and who have value in your life, be it family, friends, pets, or solitude. For me…. every day is Thanksgiving. This is what you will see if you view my photographs often. They are also my gifts. It is my gratitude journal in which I share what I appreciate."

Carol Flinn
March 25, 2018

LUSCIOUS MUSHROOMS

The art of Robin's style of photography is to take the ordinary, everyday objects of our surroundings and turn them into something extraordinary. These mushrooms were found in an open-air Farmers Market in Los Angeles, California. The pinkish-orange color, the detail of the ribs underneath, and the twisting curves exude lusciousness and sensuality.

Many people rushing through the Market, all with a purpose and intention of arriving at a destination or purchasing a specific item, may have missed the sensuality of these simple mushrooms. Robin captured it for all of us.

RIVER FLOW

This maple leaf was found floating, ever so delicately, in the Charles River near Millennium Park in Boston, Massachusetts.

> The gentle curve of the leaf,
>> The near perfect mirror reflection,
>>> The clear blue water,
>>>> The subtle sense of movement in the water ...

All add to the feeling of calm and repose in this photograph.

The leaf rests on top of the water floating with no disturbance of the river, allowing the river to carry it downstream to parts unknown. As the saying goes, sometimes it is best to not push the river ... just flow with it.

DISAPPEARING LIGHTHOUSE

Without illusion, we are left with reality … and what is that?

This photo reveals something that is not there. Is it a pillar of reflective material with a metal spiral running around the outside or is it just curved metal ribs against a cloud-filled blue sky?

Look closely and you will see the disappearing lighthouse.

LILY PAD MAGIC

Kayaking slows the pace and quiets the mind.

Gliding through the calm waters of Lake Roesiger near Snohomish, Washington, on a summer afternoon, Robin came across an unexpected field of lily pads. She paused, with intention, to deeply take in and experience the quiet serenity of the lily pads floating in the clear water.

Sometimes these unexpected moments are what create the magic in our lives, if only we take time to draw in our breath and exhale slowly.

SUNRISE ON THE ATLANTIC

Standing at sunrise on the edge of an ocean is a primordial experience … always has been, always will be.

Something about the experience of gazing at the water, listening to the waves, and feeling the sand shift beneath your feet while the water laps at your ankles makes it impossible to be anywhere except the here and now. Perhaps it is the rhythm of the waves that allows synchronization with your heartbeat … slowing it down and bringing your body's physical flow in harmony with the pull of the ocean. If you stand there long enough in the early dawn, you can lose yourself and simply be the experience. You become one with the Energy around you.

THINGS ARE NOT AS THEY SEEM

When things do not appear as we believe they should, a tension is created that demands explanation. So it is with this photo.

Because the viewer does not see the whole of the object, the photo creates an uncertainty about reality. What appears to be a shadow of the horizontal lines does not match with the lack of shadow for the vertical lines or the hanging chain.

In Robin's words, "I play on the idea that the viewer does not know what I am viewing as a whole. The viewer can then, for himself, imagine it in his or her own context. What is there is not always … in this image, you speculate that there is a shadow, however, there was no sun. It is a tiered shingled surface. You are witnessing the indentations of the wood. All can be illusion … reality is the creation of the one who perceives."

HEART LEAF WITH RAINDROPS

"In the end these things matter most:

How well did you love?

How fully did you live?

How deeply did you learn to let go?"

From the teachings of the Buddha

RAINBOW UMBRELLA

In the midst of one of those overcast, drizzly days in Seattle, this child with the rainbow umbrella paused to gaze at the Seattle Center fountain. The splash of color against the fountain's streams of water and the natural wetness from the drizzly rain created an image of joy, simplicity, and wonder.

LOVE IS LIFE

The white paint on the grey, weathered coloring of this fence of stones in Savannah, Georgia, is striking both in its presentation and in its message. The simplicity of the statement, "Love is Life," combined with the starkness of the white paint creates a powerful image. It brings the reader to the converse notion that without love, there is no life.

There is nothing that could be more true.

THE VALUE OF A MOMENT

It must have been a photographer who said, "you will know the true value of a moment when it becomes a memory." These two water drops on a pale pink leaf are on the verge of falling to the ground.

The texture of the leaf …
　　The small drop ready to slide down the curve …
　　The blurred background…

All add emphasis to the tenuousness of the moment. Robin captured this moment of suspension between clinging and falling. If you look closely, you may see her reflection.

FROZEN TIME

It was a particularly cold and harsh winter on Lake Galena in Bucks County, Pennsylvania that year. The park bench, with the frozen lake waters locking it in place and time, conveyed a sense of permanence and desolation. Where once families had gathered for Sunday picnics, there was only a stark reminder of good times past. The sounds of geese clacking, dogs barking, and children laughing had all been silenced. The air was still with no hints of fragrance from the wild flowers and forest backdrop. Only faith in the passage of time and the ever-changing seasons remained.

Robin captured the isolation and starkness of frozen time in this black and white photograph.

FALCON

This book would not be complete without a photograph of Falcon, the rescue dog that accompanied Robin on her journey of recovery. With this photograph, Robin captured Falcon's gentle soulfulness. His quiet, peaceful nature was a perfect match for Robin's penchant to stop on their walks together to take photographs. He would wait patiently by her side or romp in the grass until she was done, then travel down the path with her to the next stop.

People often commented on his eyes and the way he would gaze at them, saying "he has people eyes!" Perhaps he did … perhaps he was an old soul who found his way to Robin at the time when she needed him the most. We can only imagine what thoughts or feelings were behind those eyes. For certain, there was love, acceptance, and understanding.

Falcon will be traveling with Robin throughout eternity.

DOGWOOD MIRACLE

Flowers abound in the world. It seems the varieties, colors, and shapes are endless. Each flower has evolved perfectly to draw the best from the environment around it and produce delicate objects of incredible beauty. Robin's photos of flowers emphasize the uniqueness of each variety. In this photo of a dogwood blossom, the light and shadows dancing around the brilliant orange center herald the passage from winter to spring. This precious miracle has occurred annually without fail … a repeated sign of hope and rebirth for millions of years.

"If we could see the miracle of a single flower clearly, our whole life would change."

From the teachings of the Buddha

FOREST BATHING

The Japanese culture brings us "Shinrin-Yoku," which translates into English as "forest bathing" or "taking in the forest atmosphere." The healing properties of standing in the midst of a forest and soaking up the sights, smells, and sounds are well known.

In this photo, Robin captures the experience of forest bathing … of being present under the canopy of a living forest. The pine trees standing tall with the sun shining through allow us to slow down and appreciate things that can only be seen or heard when we move slowly. We experience heightened senses as we smell the fragrance of the pines, feel the warmth of the sun, and hear a gentle breeze rustling in the trees. The exchange of oxygen and carbon dioxide between humans and plants is a never-ending, healing interaction that benefits both species.

We are all part of a much greater whole.

CHINESE WATERCOLOR BIRDS

It was late fall on Lake Galena near Doylestown, Pennsylvania. The fog had rolled in and settled on the water like a soft blanket. All was quiet except for the incessant chatter of the geese. Robin was there in her early morning walk with Falcon. As she stood silently by the water, she watched as the geese swam below and flew through and above the fog. The clacking of the geese was almost deafening as they swarmed in and out of the fog. Robin waited patiently for just the right moment, then captured it all … the noisy circular dance of the geese, the mist of fog on the skin, and the sweetness of the morning air.

This brief moment of connection with nature quiets the mind. The sense of peace and well-being is pervasive. It is a blessing from beyond.

ALLIGATOR AND SPIDER

On a swamp tour in Louisiana, Robin was on the look out to photograph alligators. The moment this alligator surfaced out of the water, with the bayou water glistening on its head, presented Robin with the perfect shot. It was not until Robin brought the photo up on her computer that she noticed the spider nearby skating on the water's surface. The contrast of the hulking, menacing heaviness of the alligator with the light-hearted, nonchalant skating of the spider could not have been better displayed.

This unexpected addition to the photo was a reminder that chance events can result in unforeseen joy.

AFRICA

Standing on the edge of Oldepai Gorge in Tanzania, where the evolutionary trail of our shared ancestry began, is like taking a time machine to the place of our collective birth. It is a reminder that, despite the adaptations of our species to all climates of the earth and the varying cultures that have resulted across millennia, we all came from the same Mother so very long ago. To acknowledge this on a deep level is transformative.

This silhouette of an African woman against the photo effect of a sunburst captures this transformative experience. The sunburst represents the Source of our existence. The woman represents the Mother of our birth as well as the Mother of our future.

Being mindful of our beginnings is necessary to ensure our future.

CALIFORNIA CRUISING

It was summertime in Los Angeles. We were cruising in a 1968 white Cadillac Deville convertible through Hancock Park with a West Highland terrier named Margaret. Catching the sun's rays, we headed back to the '60s with the sounds of the Mamas and the Papas and the Beach Boys. Margaret was our muse as we meandered down Beverly Boulevard. The broad "land yacht" of the Cadillac transported us to a time when the Age of Aquarius promised to bring about increased harmony and spirituality on earth. All that was needed was "love, love, love."

From the back seat, Robin used her camera to capture the carefree mood and essence of the California lifestyle. Sometimes perspective makes all the difference.

BEING AWAKE

The delicate strands of a spider web on the decaying shell of a flower long gone serve as a net for perfectly formed water drops. Look closely and you will see the inverted reflection of blue sky and a single tree on a green hillside contained in each drop of water. Robin's eye for detail in this photo reminds us of life's fragility and impermanence, yet at the same time, of the power of a single water drop to contain the whole world. Against a muted background, the image brings clarity to the life sustaining force of water.

"Those who are awake live in a state of constant amazement."

From the teachings of the Buddha

WRITING ON A WALL

One can only imagine who it might have been who sat on this worn bench to write these words, "Live Slow, Die Whenever," on a brick wall.

Was it a homeless person who chose this spot to sleep one night, and then woke the next morning with this epiphany to share with the world?

Perhaps it was an elderly man taking a stroll one morning who decided to stop and write down his life's lesson.

It could have been a teenager, already too tired from life's struggles, who expressed this thought.

Robin caught the empty bench with the sun and shadows highlighting the message in white paint, leaving only the imagination to wonder about the origin and interpretation of the words.

RAISING THE SAIL

Sri Ramakrishna Paramhansa was an Indian mystic who lived in the mid-1800's on the outskirts of Calcutta. A central tenet of his teachings was that the revelation of God takes place at all times. The sailboat calls to mind one of his quotes,

> "The winds of grace are always blowing,
> but you have to raise the sail."

This photograph evokes this sentiment. While taking a walk on the beach at sunset, Robin discovered this sailboat gliding through the waters near Provincetown, Massachusetts. The sun reflecting on the sails cast a yellow glow in the calm waters, giving rise to a sense of serenity and peace. By being receptive in the moment, Robin caught the winds of grace.

STEAMBOAT PADDLES

These bright red paddles of a Mississippi River steamboat are captured against the muted background of a bridge in New Orleans. The bluish haze recalls hot, sultry days when the air is still, and the steamboat whistle draws us back to another time. The sound of traffic on the bridge jolts us back to the present. This juxtaposition of old and new is a favorite theme in Robin's photography. The simple lines of the paddles against the more elaborate construction of the bridge offer a contrast between then and now.

SERENDIPITY

The dictionary defines "serendipity" as "the occurrence and development of events by chance in a happy or beneficial way."

While taking her morning walk in Boston's Millennium Park, Robin accidentally dropped her camera. It was not until she downloaded her photos later in the day that she discovered this photo taken accidentally as the camera fell from her hands. Her free flying Einstein white hair was beautifully captured against the brilliant blue sky of a New England winter morning.

SUN RAYS

Robin's framing of sunrays beyond the darkness of shadows reminds us that, although we may walk through dark times, there will always be light and warmth on the other side. Pausing for a moment in the shadows, Robin captured this image of hope on a paved walkway in Boston's Arnold Arboretum. Beyond the light, the road forks right and left reminding us of the line from the poem by Robert Frost, "The Road Not Taken,"

> "Two roads diverged in a wood, and I took the one less traveled by, and that has made all the difference."

Out of darkness come choices, to either travel the same worn path we have always traveled or to take a new direction … to stay safe in the predictability of our past, however painful, or to face the uncertain possibility that a new course may lead to happiness. The choice is ours.

CROSSING THE BRIDGE

It was autumn when Robin and Falcon took their morning walk through Lenape Park in Perkasie, Pennsylvania. The old wooden bridge with chipped white paint crossed the stream where the geese gathered. Falcon walked ahead of Robin, then paused and looked back to make sure she was following. He waited patiently for her to take the photo and then cross the bridge with him to continue on the other side.

Robin did not realize at the time that this photo would represent Falcon's passage to another realm four years later. Falcon's physical form died in August 2017 after a fast growing cancer invaded his body, ten years after he entered Robin's life and directed her on a new path. The night after his passage, Robin asked Falcon for a sign that he was OK before she went to sleep. The next morning, this photo appeared on her Facebook Memories page.

Falcon's gift to Robin was the Essence of Love … that element which is Life Giving. What is that element? It is a spiritual connection that is self-less and unconditional. Love allows us to become Ego-less to the point of evaporation … that point when our physical form returns to energy, adds to energy, and becomes greater by joining the Eternal Whole. The energy of the spiritual connection remains imbedded in the hearts of those who have loved us and we have loved in return. This Life Giving element is then passed on to generations throughout eternity.

They say when a pet dies, they cross a Rainbow Bridge to wait on the other side. As on that old wooden bridge in Lenape Park, Falcon is there … waiting patiently.

AFTERWORD

In Pursuit of Light

With a pocket sized point and shoot camera in her hand and a Puerto Rican rescue dog named "Falcon" by her side, Robin initiated a daily practice of gratitude and contemplation to advance her recovery from depression. Medication and therapy had been her ongoing tools for years, but it was not until she found an avenue of expression through photography that she was able to recreate her life and recognize her unique talents and values. More importantly, she discovered beauty, simplicity, and light through the lens of her camera. By pursuing the light, she found her way out of the darkness.

Along the way, Robin was also inspired by Project Semicolon, a global non-profit movement founded in 2013 (Project Semicolon@projectsemicolon.com). The movement's message was simply this:

> "A semicolon is used when an author could have chosen to end their sentence, but chose not to. The author is you and the sentence is your life."

Robin identified with this message. At the age of 60, she walked into a tattoo parlor to obtain her first tattoo, a semi-colon on her right arm, as a reminder "to take a pause." She then added her own message through a second tattoo on her left arm, that of the ellipsis (dot dot dot). For her, this was her "to be continued" message to herself. Both tattoos were powerful representations of her recovery.

Robin continues to use her gift of seeing the patterns and simplicity of life as a way to bring joy to others. Her photography reminds us all to take a pause and appreciate what is in front of us, if we only seek it out with a sense of purity and gratitude.

For information about how to purchase prints of Robin's photography, contact Robin at cfr210@me.com.